Contents

Why you and I need this book

In this busy world, we all have a great many tasks to perform each day, with seemingly precious little time to get them done. This book will introduce you to the Step Method - a guaranteed method of gaining you extra time every day - starting from Day 1. The objective is to get you back on top of your workload - and stay there.

As companies and organisations seek and need to become more efficient to survive, so headcounts are being reduced, and departments and divisions merged. But there may still be the same amount of work to be done - and the remaining staff have to find a way of completing everything with fewer and fewer resources.

Sometimes this same problem can arise as the result of the business or organisation being successful. With more and more work being generated, but not enough extra staff to do it, the existing staff have to find a way to cope.

Many companies and organisations have implemented employment freezes. When members of staff leave, replacements cannot be recruited and the same problem of too much work for too few staff occurs again. Sometimes, it is not a change in circumstances that has resulted in staff not having enough time to get all the work done - it's just always been like that and everyone has to live with it.

This list is by no means exhaustive, and I'm sure there are a few situations that you'd like to add, but there is no getting away from it, falling behind with your work is a widespread and serious problem.

When it happens, you may find yourself ignoring all the tasks you know to be important, indeed vital, in favour of doing those things that are time critical. You end up rushing from one deadline to another. Strategic thinking, development of the business, or simply providing a good service go out of the window and it is very dissatisfying. In addition, it is often the case that the important things are also the most enjoyable - that's why you took the job in the first place - and there's just no time to do them.

Within companies and organisations the problem is cumulative. Work generally goes from one department to another through an organisation. If one department becomes a bottleneck, it causes problems in other departments. How many projects get delayed because someone "didn't have the time" to do their part? Incredibly, this is almost becoming an acceptable excuse for non-performance, as more and more people fall behind in their work. The more frequent expectation that "time pressure" is an acceptable excuse may be evidence of deeper management problems. The organisation is in serious trouble when people are unable to get important work completed for want of time. (And don't go thinking that prioritizing your work by importance is the answer, because it often isn't - but more of that later.)

Falling behind doesn't just have serious consequences for the organisation, but may have important ramifications for the individual(s) concerned. It is almost impossible to do a good job when you have a backlog of work and this raises problems of lack of confidence, discontentment and stress. For many reasons, top management rarely address this specific and important problem. Often they don't see that it is their responsibility to ensure that the members of their team have the time (and not just the skills) to do an effective job. Sometimes they simply don't see the harm that is being caused. In many cases the same problem is affecting them too and they don't know how to get themselves out of trouble, let alone help their team.

This is why you and I need the Step Method.

The book is not just for middle and senior managers........ in fact it's not just for managers. It is for anyone wanting to move forward in their chosen career/organisation. It works just as well for a doctor as receptionist, just as well for a warehouse assistant as his boss, just as well for a board director as a management trainee, - so don't think it doesn't apply to you. If you have a job, paid or unpaid, or a position in an organisation, then there will be times when you will have too much work to do in the time available. You may well be one of the many who are completely snowed under. You need to find a way to get back on top of your work and stay there, so that you can concentrate on the really important (and enjoyable) parts of your job, and make yourself successful.

Whilst this book is primarily aimed at solving the problems of the over- worked, the same principles apply to anyone who is looking to get more done in a given period of time. If you want to achieve more, create extra thinking time, or simply want to spend more time with your family this book will help you achieve your aims.

Over the years, I have tried many different ways of approaching and tackling this problem. The result is an easy to understand and follow, 4 Step Method to overcome the problems of too much work in too little time. The Step Method is a guaranteed way of saving you time; this will be self-evident as you move through the book. It has been implemented in many organisations and is **always** effective.

As you move through the Steps, you will discover many completely new ideas, but some of these ideas you will have already worked out for yourself (at least I hope so). Simply follow the timing and process of each step merging the new ideas with those you already know. It's not revolutionary, but it will transform your day and guarantees that you will start saving time from day 1. There is one key factor, however, that needs to be carefully monitored. Move through the book, following the steps in order. Each step will seem simple and straight forward and you will want to move on quickly. This would be a mistake. By the time you finish step 4, you will be saving hours every day, but only if you have fully mastered each step in turn - and mastering anything takes time. So it is important that you do not move through the book too quickly and that you do not attempt the next step until you feel you have mastered the one you're on. Take as much time as you need to become an expert at each step. It's not a race, it's about the best way of saving as much time as possible.

Throughout the book, practical examples are used to explain and advise how the Step Method works and how to implement it. Follow them in turn, to get maximum benefit. There is a list of the examples, with page numbers, at the end of book should you need to refresh your memory about any of the points.

Saving time communicating

Modern communication systems have transformed everyday life in general and business/organisational life in particular. We have never been so well informed, and it is quick and easy to communicate with our friends and colleagues. With computers, tablets and smart phones using email, texts and instant messaging, we should save so much time when communicating, that we all should have more leisure time every day.

So how is it that the reverse is true? We are each spending more and more time communicating with each other and it's taking up the time that we used to spend doing our job. We've all heard (and most likely said) "I came back from a week's holiday to find 300 emails in my inbox" followed by "I spent all of my first day back just answering them."

Now that virtually everyone has a mobile phone, you'd think that phone communication would be quick and easy for everyone, but the result is that we are spending more and more time on the phone. Add this to the extra time spent on emails and you find that you can't get anything done because you are on the phone and writing emails all day. It has become a modern curse and one that needs positive action to counteract it (if it's your job to be exclusively on the phone and/or writing emails, then even more reason to look at some positive action to increase your efficiency).

Another method of communicating that seems to gobble up more and more of our time is meetings. How many times have you tried to contact someone, only to be told "he's in a meeting". It's very frustrating because you've wasted time trying to get in contact, as well as wasting even more time having to now wait for your answer. Conversely, how many times have you missed someone trying to contact you because **you** were in a meeting?

Step 1 provides simple solutions to these problems, dealing firstly with phone calls and emails, then with meetings

(If you never use a telephone, email or attend meetings, skip to Step 2, which will definitely be relevant to your current situation.)

Step 1 - Phone calls and emails
Only you will know the precise amount of time you spend on the phone and emailing. If you follow a few simple rules, experience of implementing the Step method has shown that this time can normally be reduced by 10-50%. But you don't have to take my word for it. If you want proof, simply make a note of how long you spend on phone calls and emails on each of the coming few

days. Then start implementing Step 1 and time yourself again once you have mastered it. If you only achieve a 25% saving of time you have made a huge step forward, but it should be around 50%. The time you have saved is time you have gained EVERY DAY.

If you want to know your actual % time saved, or simply would like to know how long you currently spend on the phone and emailing, you may find it easier to use the chart below to monitor your current time. Keep the form (or a photocopy of it) close to your phone and computer. Enter the day number - I suggest a minimum of 3 days to get a decent average - then each time you pick up the phone or start emailing make a note of the time from your computer clock, mobile or watch in the space provided. When you switch to an activity other than phoning or emailing enter the finishing time in the relevant box. At the end of the day complete the totals at the bottom.

DAY No:	Start time	Finish time	Duration in mins.
Example:	9.06	9.45	39
Example:	10.22	12.07	105

Total minutes on phone and emailing (A)			
Total minutes in day (B)			
% time spent on phone and emailing (A) divided by (B)			%

If you don't want to know the amount of time you've saved and just want to get started using the Step Method, then simply continue implementing Step 1.

Now take five minutes and re-run in your head the last few telephone conversations you've had, and analyse what was said and what was actually achieved. Remember that these two things are totally different. The telephone call will have had an objective, usually in the form of a question. How quickly is the question put and how quickly was it answered? Give this some serious thought as you need to concentrate on what was actually achieved. How much of what was said contributed to the objective of the call and how much was irrelevant to the objective? Our aim is to recognise the objective and achieve the result in as little time as possible. You may find it easier to structure your thoughts using the following table:

Phone call with:			
Subject	Objective	Result	Time taken

Phone call with:			
Subject	Objective	Result	Time taken

Phone call with:			
Subject	Objective	Result	Time taken

You should now find it quicker and easier to establish the objective of the call. Using this information, Step 1 will now show you how to make a huge reduction in the time you spend on the phone, whilst achieving the same result.

We now turn to some of the practical Examples which explain how the Step method works and how you should start to implement it. Example 1 deals with a very common occurrence...........your telephone ringing, be it mobile or fixed line. The example shows how to save time doing this everyday activity:

Example 1. Receiving telephone calls

A colleague phones you for a piece of information. There'll be the "how are you's" on both sides, a meandering account of the information required and a few bits of gossip. Total time (say) 4 minutes.

Try this:

As soon as the phone goes and it's established who is on the phone say something like "I'm right in the middle of something - is it quick?" You'd be amazed at how quickly and succinctly their question will be put...... easily in a fraction of the time normally taken. Your answer will be expected to be quick too........so just give the answer in as few words as possible and your caller will be happy to put the phone down, lucky in the knowledge that he got his information just in time. The result? - the same has been achieved in less than half the time with the saving of two minutes.

Now the most important bit. Why be so ecstatic over saving two minutes?

The real point is that if you have (say) twenty telephone calls in a day. Do the same thing on each. Some will save only one minute, but others will save three minutes. On average in this example, you will save forty minutes every day.

You should vary your initial response so not to offend. Try:

"I've got someone with me, is it quick?" or

"Someone's coming any second, is it quick?" They all work equally well.

Take some time now to devise some phrases that suit your personality that will achieve the same result. Write them down because they are important. You can use this chart:

Selection of responses to incoming calls:
1. I'm right in the middle of something, is it quick?
2. I've got someone with me, is it quick?
3. Someone's coming any second, is it quick?
4.
5.
6.
7.

Remember that I said that this could apply to the vast majority of calls. If you need to establish a specific relationship with a colleague, then stay on the phone and chat. Also, this NEVER applies to talking to customers, who get all the time they require.

At this early stage in implementing the Step Method it is important to stress that saving time is not the same as cutting corners. The Step Method is a guaranteed method of saving you time, but if you start cutting corners you will simply use up this new-found time putting right what you didn't do correctly in the first place. To improve your efficiency the same calibre of work must be done in a shorter period of time. This is why it is important to focus on the **objective** of the phone call and ensure that in half the time you cover everything that needs to be said to achieve that objective.

In most cases your caller simply wants an answer to a question. It is very important to keep in mind this point about your quality of work as you go through the Steps. We shall return to this subject later, but for the time being do not accept that quicker means a lowering of quality.

The next time your phone rings have your response ready (the one in the example: "I'm right in the middle of something, is it quick" is as good as any place to start) and concentrate on giving your answer in as few words as possible. The Step method is not a theoretical exercise, but a practical method to be used straight away. "I'll start tomorrow" is not an option - get stuck in straight away (or after the period taken to time your current activity if you choose to do that). It normally works first time, but no matter if it doesn't, just give it another try next time the phone goes. Once mastered, it never fails to save significant amounts of time.

You have started on your mission to catch up with your workload, and there's no looking back. Step 1 continues with making telephone calls, as opposed to receiving them. Example 2 shows how to approach this activity and save even more time:

Example 2. Making telephone calls

You make a phone call for some information from a colleague. They key thing is to start by saying something like: "Morning John........just a quick one......." and ask your question. He knows you want to be quick and will give you a more succinct answer than he otherwise would have and you've avoided all the chit chat. End with something like "thanks a lot......we'll catch up later" and ring off. The result: another two minutes saved.

As with the receipt of calls, you can vary your wording, but the result will always be the same. You could try "Hope you're well...........I just need to know.........." ending with "I've got to get this finished.......speak later" Vary your wording to suit your personality. Again, take some time to write down some suitable phrases, and use them:

Selection of opening phrases when making a telephone call:
1. Morning (say) John.........just a quick one........
2. Hope you're well.........I just need to know........
3.
4.
5.
6.
7.

Selection of closing phrases to end a telephone call:
1. Thanks a lot.........we'll catch up later
2. I've got to get this finished........speak later

3.	
4.	
5.	
6.	
7.	

This all seems very simple, and it is, except you'd be amazed how difficult it is to always implement it. In the beginning you will constantly have to keep reminding yourself to do it. We are all so used to the slow speed and pace of conversations that you will all too easily slip back in to your old ways. It will take you some time to remember to do it for every call you make and every call you receive. In fact it usually takes some weeks before it becomes second nature, which is what you're ultimately trying to achieve. I've known people forget completely for a few days and only resume after a gentle reminder.

When you first start, colleagues and friends may catch the different way you make and answer calls, but the majority will not even notice. If anyone comments, then the truth is always the best policy. Simply explain that you're snowed under with work and are trying to catch up. Pretty soon, everyone will come to expect your phone calls to be short and to the point, and realise that you are not being cold towards them. In fact it's very interesting watching the reaction of your colleagues. The smart ones will see the benefits and start copying you. At this early stage, after only a few days, you will definitely have saved a considerable amount of time. The question is what to do with it? And the answer is: whatever you like !! You may just want to go home a bit earlier and surprise your partner but my recommendation is that you make a start at reducing the number of items on your "to do" list. Remember that the immediate objective is to get on top of your work, and then stay there. This means your extra time could be utilised directly on this objective. If you have some telephone calls to make on your "to do" list you get the double advantage of finally getting round to making the call, AND doing it in half the time.

As with Example 1, run through your wording for Example 2 in your head and use it on the next call you make. Do it now. The sooner you get started the easier it will become. Your ultimate objective is for the Step Method to become your automatic default response, requiring no extra conscious thought. This will certainly happen provided you keep doing it and it will soon become second-nature.

We are only part way through step 1 and I hope you are starting to see that it may just be possible that you are going get on top of your workload - and stay there. There's plenty more to come.

We now turn to the time we spend on emails. Example 3 addresses the Step Method's approach to the issue of how to deal with incoming mail:

Example 3. Receiving emails

You receive a request from a colleague by email - the sender wants to visit another colleague and needs to know if it's OK with you. You can reply as follows:

Dear John

Thanks for your email regarding visiting Frank. I think it's a good idea, so please go ahead.

Give him my regards, Peter

Very quick and efficient, and you've covered everything required in just a couple of minutes. Some people would string it out a bit adding some non- relevant points, but this is a pretty standard response. But what if you reply with:

OK by me.

or even:

yes.

You must ask yourself the same question as you do with telephone calls. What is the objective? In this case the recipient just wants your agreement, so there is no practical difference between the three answers - they all achieve the same result.

You just saved yourself another minute, and multiply this by the number of emails you send/receive each day and you get a remarkable saving of time. This extra time is in **addition** to the savings achieved on phone calls. Step 1 will save you a lot of time EVERY day..................just what you wanted.

With every email you send or receive, you need to ask yourself the following question:

"How can I ask the question (or give an answer) in the least number of words to get the same result?"

The vast majority of your emails don't have to be pretty, they just have to achieve their objective. As with phone calls, emails to customers do not fall into this category. Customers get every word the best you can make it, however long it takes. Some other important emails come into this same category, but Step 1 thinking deals with the majority of emails that keep our daily lives going.

Instant (internet) messaging has gone some way towards making typed messages more efficient, being a hybrid of text messaging and emailing. It seems to be perfectly acceptable to shorten words and sentences when instant messaging, in a way that has never happened for the more popular email. I do recommend this form of communication, but it has one major drawback - few people currently use it, so few people monitor their incoming messages. If you know like-minded individuals who use instant messaging, it can be a valuable tool.

One final thought before moving on - don't forget the final few words of the question above i.e. "to get the same result". As with phone calls, it is important to remember that saving time does not equate to lowering of quality.

Example 4 looks at the other big user of our time, the sending of emails and shows how the Step Method can and will save you time:

Example 4. Sending emails

You need to invite a colleague to a meeting. Your email goes something like:

Hi John

We're having a meeting at 4.00pm today to discuss last week's sales. Geoff will be presenting to the sales team the results and the whole team will be present. You won't have to give a presentation, but I think it would be wise for someone in your department to be there to be aware of the Sales Department's feelings on how things are going. The meeting is scheduled to finish at 5.00pm. I hope you can make it. Please come back to me and let me know if you can come, and if not who will deputise for you. The meeting will be held in Conference Room 4 on the second floor, and I will be attending.

It will be good to catch up with you,

Regards

Peter

All the salient points are there. It's quite a complicated mail because there are many aspects about the meeting that John needs to know about before the meeting starts. But how about:

Hi John

I'm meeting with the sales team in Conf. Rm. 4 between 4 and 5 today (Geoff presenting) to discuss last week's sales. It's best if you are there to observe, but if not, let me know who will deputise for you. Tks. Peter

Again, we ask ourselves the same question - what is the objective of the email and how can I say it in as few words as possible? All the salient points are there in both emails, so the result will be the same. Don't forget that you cannot cut corners. In this example, if you leave out an important piece of information in the email, then all the time you saved will be taken up by John having to call you to find out what he needs to know.

You must order your thoughts before you start typing, and keep it simple. It will take some time before this becomes second-nature, so in the mean time you will have to make a conscious effort to approach any email in this new way.

You now have some more saved time in the kitty , to be added to that already accumulated. As with telephone calls, colleagues will soon come to expect emails that are short and to the point, and come to appreciate it. The reason is easy to see. I'm sure that everyone can name someone in their organisation who always sends long and convoluted emails, and your heart sinks when you see one in your inbox. Your emails will have the opposite effect, with recipients knowing your email will be short and to the point.

We have already mentioned instant messaging and its advantages. Whilst using short phrases instead of long sentences is already taking place, Step 1 brings the added dimension to instant messaging of establishing the real objective of the message quickly and responding appropriately.

As with the phone calls, there is an extra advantage to the organisation of following Step 1. If it takes you significantly less time to type a shorter email, then it will take the recipient less time to read it. Similarly if you are on the phone for a lesser period of time, then a colleague on the other end of the line will also be spending less time. There is no point in trying to measure the time saving effect for your colleagues, our objective is to get **you** up to date, not them, but it is a definite plus for the organisation.

Step 1 - Meetings

Whole books have been written on the problem of excessive time spent attending meetings - a subject which is varied and complex. I, however, am going to limit myself to just one idea, which is a key part of Step 1 and will help enormously in your objective of getting on top of your workload.

Meetings can be incredibly time consuming, sometimes boring, and may not achieve what they set out to achieve. Occasionally you will attend a meeting that achieves the objective efficiently but they are few and far between. Sometimes it is vital, even enjoyable to get everyone round a table (or on a conference call) to thrash out a problem, but it must be done efficiently. One single factor that will achieve this is to appoint a chairperson. Start with yourself for your own meetings and follow the procedure below.

The chairperson should write the invitation to the meeting, thinking carefully about whom to invite, keeping the number of people to the absolute minimum, because each extra non-essential participant will increase the length of the meeting and reduce its focus. Remember there are many colleagues who are all too happy to attend meetings to justify their existence and who generate a lot of heat and very little light.

The invitation should state who will be present, the objective of the meeting and the time it will start and finish. Add that you will start promptly at the time stated.

Ensure that you start the meeting on time, or at the very latest a couple of minutes after the time you stated, and under no circumstances deviate from this rule.

At your first meeting, many will not believe you that you intend to start on time. If the majority have not arrived on time, cancel the meeting and re- schedule. I've done this several times in different companies and those arriving late to an empty room generally feel embarrassed. They won't do it again.

People will soon get the message that your meetings always start on time and that the meeting will start without them if they are late. Usually it won't be long before everyone will arrive on time, thus saving you, and everyone else, valuable minutes.

Having started on time, the chairperson must keep an eye on the clock throughout the meeting. If you are to finish on time, and you **will** finish on time, the chairperson will have to constantly be aware of how the meeting is progressing towards your stated objectives.

Chairing a meeting is a bit like hosting a dinner. As host it's your responsibility to ensure that the conversation is not dominated by those who like the sound of their own voice, and that no-one is left out who will have a valid contribution. You make sure that tempers remain on an even keel. You even ensure that the room is at the right temperature and that everyone is comfortable.

The most important task of the chairperson is to achieve the objective of the meeting by keep things relevant. Too many meetings spend a long time discussing points that are important to persons around the table but are not relevant to the meeting's objective. It is the chairperson's job to recognise this quickly and move the conversation onto the job in hand. He/she must swiftly and skilfully guide the conversation towards reaching the objective. This is key to a successful meeting and sometimes surprisingly difficult to achieve. It's because the irrelevant topics will be of interest and importance to the chairperson too, but he/she must remain completely focused on the objective of the meeting. Some people may have to be cut short, while others need to be encouraged to contribute, all the time keeping an eye on the clock and moving things towards a satisfactory conclusion. By doing this, the chairperson will achieve an on-time resolution of the objective.

Follow the points above at your next meeting and give yourself an honest assessment after it's finished. Identify thought, you will automatically make phone calls short, emails concise and meetings quick and relevant. When you reach this point, and only then, you could remove your secret item from your desk.

Step 1 concludes with a concept that is key to maximising the benefits of the Step Method.

It is very important to understand how your body, and especially your brain, works. Everyone is different and it's important you know how you tick. You need to know, or work out if you don't already know, when you work at maximum efficiency.

Take me for example. When I was younger, and I needed to get a volume of good work done, I would work from midnight until 3am with brilliant clarity of thought. I did my best work at this time, working at peak efficiency.

If I tried to do this today, the result would be hopeless; my body-clock has changed.

Now, if I need some serious thought and very efficient work, I would get up at 6.00am, be in the office by 7.00am and will have completed most of the work before everyone else gets into the office.

You need to do the tasks that need creative thinking when your mind is at its freshest, be it in the morning, afternoon, evening or night-time. This will have a huge impact on your efficiency and consequently your output.

You need to work out when your brain is at its most productive and make sure you use this time to work out your most difficult questions and problems. If you miss-time it, you will find yourself taking hours to work out something that you could have done in minutes in your productive period.

Conversely, if I had reports to wade through, or things that needed time but little creative thinking, then I would put them to one side and do them in the afternoons, when my efficiency dropped.

Take some time and think about this seriously. You can fill in the chart below to aid your thoughts. Think clearly and objectively about how your body works. When can you digest information quickly? When do you find it difficult to think creatively?

Time	Enter relevant number: 1. Most Productive 2. Quite Productive 3. Not too Productive 4. Least Productive
6.00 - 9.00 am	
9.00 - 11.00 am	
11.00 am - 1.00 pm	
1.00 - 2.00 pm (lunch?)	
2.00 - 3.00 pm	
3.00 - 6.00 pm	
6.00 - 10.00pm	
After 10.00 pm	

Using this information, plan your day to maximise your productivity.

You should also bear in mind that not every day is the same. You may find that one morning (perhaps after a late night) you find it difficult to think quickly. When this happens, don't persevere with difficult problems, switch to the time consuming stuff, otherwise your efficiency will drop dramatically. And vice versa, if you normally don't function well in the mornings, but one morning your brain is on fire, switch to solving your most difficult problems. You will work efficiently and get a lot of good work done.

One other, quite separate, thought - whether you're more efficient in the mornings or not - it's my experience that if you are currently working from 9.00am to 6.00pm, you will get more work done if you keep the number of hours the same, but switch to 8.00am to 5.00pm. That first hour in the office, before the phone starts to ring or people start interrupting you, will probably be the most efficient of the day, and will consequently dramatically affect your overall daily output.

Others will see the effect it has on your workload and will follow suit by starting early too - but the amazing thing is that they will keep themselves to themselves and get through their own work without interrupting you. They will see the benefits and increase their own efficiency.

But, most importantly, make sure you don't fall into the trap of starting earlier and still regularly staying late.

Having worked out the periods when you are most productive, here is an extra technique to extend these periods and improve the quality of your thinking process.

In just about every book on management you will get to the chapter about the importance, indeed the absolute necessity, to prioritize your work by making sure that the most important jobs get done.

The whole point of the Step Method is to get you to the point where you are on top of your workload, and therefore have no need to prioritize. You will reach this point at some stage as you go through the Steps. But until that time comes, from time to time, the level of work may rise to the point where you become completely swamped.

When this happens, it is often beneficial **not** to do the most important things first. Most people can keep a large number of things in their heads at any one time. But we all have a limit, and when we reach that limit our thinking goes haywire because we cannot keep control of everything. Your efficiency will plummet. Let's pick a figure (any figure will do because everyone has different abilities) and say we can deal with 30 problems at any one time. When you reach 31, you start to lose control. **Don't prioritize by importance,** just take the 10 problems that can be done the quickest and get them off your desk as quickly as possible. This will clear your head and you can return to working at peak efficiency. It works well, but remember that we are talking here only about those times when your brain goes into overload.

There will often be times when this is not appropriate, for example if you have an emergency that has critical ramifications,(or simply that your boss wants something immediately) and you must follow your own judgment about these situations. But if it's just your everyday tasks that have mounted up, try it.

Conclusion

Implementing Step 1 gives immediate results on day 1, and continues to gain you extra time as you become more proficient. Practice using it daily, and keep the secret item on your desk to keep things moving along. I will have proved to you that it is perfectly possible to cut by 10 - 50% the time taken on the phone and answering emails, plus a further reduction in the time you spend in meetings. If you decided to measure the time taken before you started the Step Method, then you will have your actual % time saved.

There are even better ideas in the later steps, and Step 1 will give an excellent base upon which to build. Proficiency in Step 1 will make the future steps more useful to you.

Before we move on to Step 2, I would like to discuss the ultimate aims of the Step Method. Step 1 has given you just a glimpse of how much time can be saved. Step 2 will consolidate this position while steps 3 and 4 will take you to a completely new level. I am going to suggest to you that there are people around who could do exactly the same quality and amount of work as you do in a day, always be on top of their workload, and they would only need to work half a day - that's right, they would be able to work at twice the rate that you currently achieve. I've seen it done many times and I've done it myself. It sounds incredible, if not unbelievable, but by the time you are proficient in all 4 steps, you will be able to see that this is perfectly possible. You will be able to assess your progress as you go through the Steps.

Move on now to Step 2 which will show you how to create even more time.

Remember

At the beginning I stated that it is best to master the step you're on before moving on to the next one.

Ask yourself:
– am I questioning every phone call?
– am I questioning every email?
– am I chairing meetings effectively?
– am I saving at least an hour a day?

If the answer to any of these questions is "no" then spend time concentrating on Step 1 before moving on to Step 2.

Finding a quicker way without sacrificing quality

We've dealt with the time taken on phone calls, emails and meetings. These take up a considerable part of our time, but what about the rest of the day? During this time we all do a myriad of different tasks and the problem we still face is that even when we take into consideration the time savings of Step 1, there is still not enough time in our day to get on top of our workload. Sometimes people are behind with their work at certain times of the week or month, as workload fluctuates, but it is more common to be behind for the majority or all of the time - and this is a serious issue for both the individual and their company/organisation.

Saving time doing our everyday tasks is a more difficult problem to solve than that of Step 1 owing to the diverse nature of the activities undertaken. Added to that, we have all got a speed and rhythm of work which we have developed over time, and it is very difficult to break this rhythm. We are also conditioned by the speed at which our colleagues work, either consciously or subconsciously.

Additionally, we all have an existing approach to the way we tackle problems and everyday tasks. It's mostly sub-conscious, and if asked how they approach problems, most people would find it difficult to give an answer. Clearly they spend all day at work but rarely analyse **how** they work. Most of us rarely question this because it seems so natural to work the way we have always worked. All these things combine to make it difficult to improve the situation and change the status quo.

The solution is to find a way to approach our everyday tasks that will make us more efficient. Step 2 widens the question to ask how we should approach any activity, be it problematic or simply our day-to-day workload.

We said that Step 1 would save us 10-50% of the time spent on phone calls, emails and meetings. Step 2 will also bring similar savings to the time taken doing your other tasks.

Step 2 requires you to ask yourself **the same key question** every time you are required to do **any activity**. It's always the same question, and it is:

"Is there a quicker way of dealing with this without sacrificing quality?"

It's just twelve words, and they may seem simplistic, but their significance is key to achieving your objective - and when answered will dramatically transform your day. We rarely, if ever, ask ourselves this question, we just do what comes naturally, or more often just follow the way we've acted before. This question requires us to

- Do I need to be doing this activity when my brain is at its most (or least) productive?
- How can I say the same thing in fewer words?

Before, you had no need to seek a quicker way of doing something, so you never found one. But now you have; and it's amazing how the brain reacts when pushed. You will find the process getting easier and easier as you get more practice.

Remember that sometimes you won't be able to find an effective, quicker way and that's fine - just complete it as you would normally and move on to the next task. Sometimes you'll save no time, sometimes a little time and sometimes a lot of time, but the overall effect will see you well on the way to getting on top of your workload.

If you find that you are just not coming up with new, quicker ways of doing things (unusual but by no means rare) then you must take care not to fall even further behind with your work because you are spending a lot of time trying to implement Step 2. If this is the case, then just choose 1 task, and ask yourself all the questions listed above in turn. Eventually you will find an answer to your question: "Is there a quicker way of dealing with this without sacrificing quality?" For the first week, just choose one task per day. On the second week, choose two tasks per day, on the third week three and so on.

Sometimes there may be safety issues or security issues to be considered. These must be given due consideration, but it does not preclude you from giving the full Step 2 treatment, because your question includes "without sacrificing quality".

Some people maintain that there is always a direct correlation between quality and speed - the concept being that if you do something more quickly there must be an automatic lowering of quality. I take issue with this view and have personally disproved it. Many of the examples in this book show that it is perfectly possible to achieve a quicker result without loss of quality. But don't be complacent, and keep a close eye on it. Occasionally you may think of a much quicker way of doing something but realise that the result will be a definite lowering of quality. Your immediate reaction should be to try to find a solution **without** the lowering of quality. If you cannot, then here you must make a judgement call about the trade off between speed and quality and every single case is different - only you can make that call. But these cases should and must remain the exception. Do not fall in to the trap of only thinking of quicker ways that diminish quality. In the vast majority of cases only accept the quicker way if it maintains quality. This **must** and will become your default setting but you should watch this carefully.

As with Step 1, there follows a series of examples describing and explaining how Step 2 works in practice. Don't forget that you should be content to save a couple of minutes on each action as they will soon mount up. The first example shows how to approach the weekly compiling of a set of figures. This example has been chosen because the same approach could be used for the compiling of any regular report. It gives suggestions of the type of questions you should ask yourself in order to find a quicker way without sacrificing quality.

Example 5. Re-thinking regular tasks (1)

Every week, it's your job to compile a set of figures for your boss/colleagues/team. It's always in the same layout, with the same details, and takes you about an hour.

Ask yourself:

– Are all the figures used by whomever uses the report? My experience is that some are never used but no-one ever questioned it.

– Are some of the figures already on another report? If so it might be much quicker to add some extra details to that report, rather than starting from scratch every week.

– Would it be quicker to present it in a different format? Perhaps it would be quicker in excel rather than the company's bespoke computer system (remember to keep within your company's rules regarding computer generated reports).

– Are the figures read every week? You'd be surprised how many reports lie unread. Perhaps you could suggest every fortnight, or every month, and each report would then be read and digested.

It would be almost impossible not to save some time when you question things in this way.

The important thing is to follow this approach for everything you do. You complete so many tasks that if you only saved an average of 2 minutes on each (and many years of implementing the Step Method shows it may well be more), it will have a major effect on your day.

The next example takes another regular activity - filing, and shows the type of questions you could ask yourself in order to help you find a successful Step 2 solution.

Example 6. Rethinking regular tasks (2)

We all have to file away our paper documents (and remember that filing is a retrieval system not a storage system).

Ask yourself:

– You've always filed away document A - but does anyone ever need them?

Perhaps the bin would be more appropriate instead of your filing pile.

– Isn't document B always held on computer, so why save a paper copy when in the rare event that a paper copy is required it could easily be re-printed? By way of example, and proof, most companies keep a hard copy of every customer invoice that they raise. This includes my own company. I recently enacted Step 2 thinking (we are all constantly improving) and sent a one line email to the outside auditor asking if I really needed to keep a hard copy - bearing in mind copies are always held on the computer. The reply said that it was not a requirement. Not having to keep copy invoices has made a tremendous saving in paper, ink cartridges, storage space (for 7 years!!) and more importantly in the time taken to file them.

– Don't they keep copies of document C in the accounts dept? Again, in the rare event of needing a copy you could copy theirs.

I stated above that filing is retrieval system and not a storage system and many people forget or ignore this. Lack of thought about your filing system is one of the main wastes of time in every organisation. You may be the exception that proves the rule, but if you are like most people, you would be horrified if you added up the time you spent in a week looking for bits of paper, or trying to find a computer document (even with modern search engines). A bit of time spent working out the most sensible system, and a bit of extra time ensuring you file everything in the right place will save you a lot of time in the long run.

Remember, it's not the single action saving of time, but the cumulative effect that will give you the result you require.

The Step 2 question is: "Is there a quicker way of dealing with this without sacrificing quality?". You will notice that it doesn't say "**You** must find a quicker way.................." which means that occasionally you could ask your colleagues for their thoughts. Another person often comes at the problem from a different angle and will come up with ideas that you would never have thought of. You are not replacing your thoughts with theirs, rather adding their thoughts to yours to give a more complete solution. In the next example, you can see this in action (and if you work in a warehouse it may also give you a few ideas):

Example 7. Rethinking repetitive tasks

I was once sent to help out in the warehouse of a medium sized company. There was a manual picking and packing operation which had got behind with the shipping of orders and this poor service level was starting to adversely affect the reputation of the business. I pitched in, picking and packing, and did my bit to help reduce the backlog.

On the third day, I was having lunch with the pickers and asked them why they thought there was such a backlog of orders. They had no idea - in fact it had never occurred to them to question why. They (in their own words) just did the picking. I asked them if they could think of any way of speeding up the operation. I had trouble keeping up with their replies. They had plenty of ideas about how their job could be made easier (not quite the same thing, but the result is exactly the same), but no-one ever asked them. I listened to what they had to suggest. One result was that a different style of trolley was used to pick the orders which meant that more products could be picked on each picking journey. There was no additional cost because the new trolley was the same price as the old design. The products were re-laid in a different order in the warehouse so that the average picking journey was shorter (and therefore quicker). This resulted in more orders being picked per hour.

When I spoke to the packers, they said that if the storage area for the packing boxes could be relocated closer to their packing benches then they wouldn't have to waste so much time replenishing their supplies of boxes. In this case I suggested we go one better by having at least one complete day's supply of boxes kept at each packing station so that we would eliminate the need for the packers to leave their packing station to replenish supplies.

Not only did I not come up with the sound Step 2 solutions, these pickers and packers liked the fact that their ideas were listen to and acted upon. Whilst it is true that managers and directors have more opportunity to implement the Step Method, anyone in an organisation could and should be thinking in this way.

Every company is different, every organisation is different, with a different set of personalities managing and working there. The important thing is for you to act as an individual. Normally, your brain will react positively and you'll be surprised at what you come up with just by starting to think in this different way. But if you need to give yourself a little nudge to get going, refer to the list of questions on Page 37 at any time. I would encourage you to add a few questions to this list that are applicable to your own situation, and have the list easily available for reference.

Get started straight away. Very few people think like this but it will become second nature - you won't have to constantly force yourself, but until that time comes you only have to keep asking yourself that key question: "Is there a quicker way of doing this without sacrificing quality?" No other magic formula is required, just the question.

By way of a further explanation, it's a bit like reading a map. You don't do it very often, but when you do, you ask yourself the question:"What's the quickest way from A to B?" No-one needs to tell you how to do it, you have all the information you need. Your brain just swings into action and you do it. And the more you do it, the quicker and more proficient you become. The Step Method works in exactly the same way. Just follow what comes naturally and you'll be able to do it. Sometimes when reading a map you may want to find the prettiest way, rather than the fastest. That's absolutely fine if you have the time available. The Step Method address those who need to find the quickest, time-saving route. You will then be in a position to really reap the benefits that come from the addition of Step1 and Step 2. At the very least you will be much closer to being completely up to date with your work, if not there already.

As with Step 1, Step 2 is not a theoretical exercise, but a practical Method to be used daily. Hopefully you've started to ask yourself the Step 2 question, and have started to come up with solutions.

Step 2 should be used to speed up both your regular activities as well as one-off problems. Example 10 describes a common problem in companies and organisations: occasional peaks in workload which produce bottlenecks. The example is going to describe one such problem and then invite you to have a shot at quickly finding a solution. It's highly unlikely you will guess the eventual outcome, but the object of the example is to get you thinking of quick ways of resolving problems. You may well come up with a better resolution than our man did here.

If you can quickly come up with an acceptable answer, then make a note of it in the box provided and read on to see the eventual solution arrived at. If you can't think of anything appropriate, then look again at the list of questions you should ask yourself on Page 37, and see if this prompts a solution.

If you don't come up with anything, that's fine, because we've already said that sometimes you'll save a lot of time and sometimes you won't. But it will definitely start you thinking in the right direction and it will only be a matter of time before you start coming up with Step 2 solutions to difficult problems.

Example 8. Re-thinking occasional peaks in business or work

Good managers are generally prepared for peaks and troughs in the quantity of work required, but occasionally there is a sudden rise in workload that had not been predicted. Step 2 thinking will have you trying to think of quick ways of dealing with the sudden rush of work. Sometimes, however, there is nothing for it but to hire some temporary staff, especially if the work is of a manual nature.

The warehouse manager of a company I worked for had the matter in hand by having not one but two methods of coping with this situation. The first was to ensure that all the warehouse staff were regularly moved around to work in different sections of the warehouse. This meant that if a bottleneck occurred in one section, he could easily swing staff in from the other sections to clear the backlog. This is a technique that I would thoroughly recommend as it incurs no extra cost and members of staff get the added benefit of having a variety of tasks, instead of just doing the same thing day in day out. His back-up to this was to have good contacts with not one but three temp agencies. He could always find the staff he needed.

All was well until a nationwide promotion produced more orders than his staff and the temps could handle. No more temps were available and the orders were mounting up and customers were complaining that they were not getting their promotional stock. He needed a solution fast.

What is your solution?

The chosen solution:

We started discussing the problem when the warehouse manager went quiet for a while - a sure sign he was thinking hard - and then he came up with "I bet everyone's got a son/daughter/spouse /friend/ acquaintance/ neighbour who'd love a extra few pounds". He immediately sent a message to all staff with the request. Before the close of play that day, he had more names than he could handle, and asked for the requisite number to come the following morning. Not only did he have enough staff, but also had three added, key advantages. He had a major cost saving in no longer having to pay the high agency fees. Staff members were happy because one of their relatives (or friends) was earning money and lastly the not inconsiderable advantage of having a pool of casual workers, who over the years, built up their levels of experience.

He'd been a warehouse manager for years, but had never come up with this idea before - which just goes to show that you should never stop applying Step 2 thinking and trying to find a quicker way.

Helpful pointers and other examples

In Step 1 and Step 2, we have discussed the fact that saving time does not mean cutting corners, and of course the same applies to all the steps. There are other negative factors affecting efficiency which are just as relevant and just as important, and it is crucial that all this time you are saving does not adversely affect the organisation in other areas.

As we saw in the previous examples (and it is just as relevant in an office) if there is a bottleneck of work in a department, it takes only 2 seconds to say "get 5 temps in and clear the backlog". The problem will be resolved and it only took you 2 seconds to find the solution. If the situation is desperate, and must be sorted out immediately, then under certain circumstances this may be the best thing to do - but usually the same Step 2 thinking will reveal several, more cost effective ways to resolve the problem.

The same applies to security, in all its forms. For example you may have a problem having someone to stay behind at the end of the day to back-up your server. Again, 2 seconds thought will tell you that if you do it once a week instead of daily, then you will have resolved the problem, and some people will go for this option. Step 2 thinking would rarely advocate this solution as we must not "sacrifice quality" and the cost of replacing lost files would easily out-weigh the extra cost (in time or money) of having someone stay behind every day to do the back-ups.

Always remember the Step 2 question: What is the quickest way of doing this **without sacrificing quality.** The last three words are highlighted here to emphasise the important point that saving time and efficiency are different things (efficiency being defined as the ability to achieve more work of equal quality in a given period of time). The majority of your Step 2 thinking will automatically save time without the sacrificing of quality, but be aware that on certain decisions, you may be placing an unacceptable burden on the organisation. Watch out for:

- The saving of time in your department simply increasing the time required in another department
- The saving of your time, simply increasing the time required by someone else in your own department (training excluded)
- Have you exposed your company to any security lapses?
- Have you exposed your company to any competitive dangers? You should add to this list any dangers that your particular organisation faces.

Another useful pointer when getting to grips with Step 2 is that if nothing new springs to mind when you trying to find a quicker way, you could try asking yourself a related question that may point you in the right direction:

"Why is the task normally done this way?"

If your answer is the most common one, it will be: "I don't know". This means the task is wonderfully positioned for you to be successful with your follow-up main question of "What is the quickest way of dealing with this without sacrificing quality?" If you haven't asked yourself "why is it done this way?" before, then the chances are no-one else has and it's very likely you'll be able to find that quicker way.

Often the answer you get to the question "Why is it done this way" is the worst possible answer of all, which is "because we always do it this way". If your answer is this, then it's highly likely you're going to find a quicker way and save a considerable amount of time. You'd be amazed at how many actions in an organisation are done because they've always been done like that. People rarely sit back and question why. I'm sure you've worked out why. It's because they've got their heads down trying to get on top of their workload.

Working from home

We now move to assessing how the Step Method works for those who spend part or all of their time working from home.

The answer is that the entire Step Method is equally relevant to those working in either environment. In theory there should be no difference and all the benefits should be the same. In practice, however, the results are often very different for those working at home, for one specific reason.

With no travelling time to and from work, being at home should mean that it's much easier to stay on top of your workload. The reality, however, is that the opposite may well be true owing to one single factor - the high level of distraction experienced at home. The Step Method will work just as well from home, as long as it is implemented fully.

Offices and factories are busy places, with constant interruptions to your concentration, but the distraction experienced at home is of a different type and intensity. When you're at home family members (although they will have been told otherwise) always feel that you are available to talk to them. Friends will phone you, or pop in. There are always jobs that need doing straight away. Combine these together and you find that when you are doing your work, you can work quickly and efficiently - the problem is that you don't get much chance to do your work. The Step Method won't have a chance to transform your life because of the constant and lengthy interruptions.

The best way of ensuring that you overcome this problem is to:

a) Move your desk to a room where you can close the door and everyone in the house knows that when the door is closed, you need to be left alone.
b) Define the periods of time that you need to work and stick to them.
c) Explain to family and friends (again) that you must get your work done and that you need to be left alone to do it.
d) Ensure you have a telephone (mobile or fixed) that is on your desk and not in another room.
e) If you need a constant supply of hot or cold drinks, take a flask in with you.

If you find yourself working from home (or members of your team work from home) make sure you understand that it is very difficult to get your work done and that

you must make positive moves to ensure efficient working practices. I learned this very early on in my career.
When on the road selling, I used to get strange looks
from my neighbours because after a long day's selling
I would get home and sit on the drive in my car for three
quarters of an hour before going through the front door.
I needed to collate my orders and do the paperwork.
I knew that as soon as I stepped in through the door, the
paperwork would never get done as my wife and kids
needed immediate attention (they were often waiting for
me to get home to give me things to do !!). The strange
looks were worth it- my paperwork was always completed
on time and I could enjoy my evenings.

We finish Step 2 with an additional idea that does
not directly answer the Step 2 question, but uses a form
of Step 2 thinking. It will certainly help you get on top
of your workload:

Example 9. Finishing everything before going on holiday

We've all been there - sitting at our desks at 9.00 in the evening the day before going on holiday, trying to finish everything and not quite making it. This happened to me several times before I turned to a form of Step 2 thinking to provide a solution. I need to find the quickest way of completing everything before I went on holiday.

Try this simple trick. Start the final week before your holiday (or a long business trip) telling yourself that on the final day you will be leaving at lunchtime. Gear your week to not being there on the final afternoon, arranging appointments accordingly.

If you try your best to finish by lunchtime on your final day, then by 5.00pm, you will have just about completed every last thing that you needed to do, and can go away with a peaceful mind.

Playing tricks with yourself is unusual, but this does work.

Conclusion

Step 2 is a powerful tool. It centres around just one simple question: Is there a quicker way of dealing with this without sacrificing quality? It's simple and straight forward to understand, but it does necessitate a change of approach and a change of thinking. As you become more proficient, so the time you save will become greater.

We are now half way through the steps and you should really be starting to feel the difference in your working day. When you add the time savings from Step 1 to those of Step 2 you will begin to appreciate this.

Move on now to Step 3 where you will find more new ideas to ensure you get back on top of your workload - and stay there.

Remember:

At the beginning I stated that it is best to master the step you're on before moving on to the next one.

Ask yourself:

– do I try to think of the quickest way of doing every action?

– do I do it every day?

– am I saving a least an hour a day by using step 2 (in addition to the hour saved every day using step 1)? If the answer to any of these questions is "no" then spend time concentrating on Step 2 before moving on to Step 3

Eliminating tasks completely

You remember my statement about there being people around who could do everything you do, but in half the time? Steps 1 and 2 have given us a glimpse that this may be possible - but on their own, the Steps so far will not have propelled you to this level. We've saved huge amounts of time, but it's just not enough and we need some new ideas to help us achieve this aim. So what new technique can we utilise to help propel us to this level?

You are already finding quicker and quicker ways of doing your tasks, and you may be one of the most efficient employees in your organisation, so how is it possible take it to a new level? Step 3 , just like Step 2 entails you asking yourself just one simple question:

"How can I reduce the time taken to zero?"

Don't find a quicker way of doing it - find a way of not having to do it at all. Bizarre as it may seem, there are many things that you are paid to do, that need take no time at all - not just one or two things - there are lots.

At the heart of Step 3 is your ability to recognise what any particular task **needs to achieve**. Once you've established this (and it's quick enough to do) you must ask yourself if the way you would normally deal with this task achieves the required result. Normally the answer is yes, but your thought process is the same whether the answer is yes or no. You need to examine the task and ask yourself if the result (not the action) is already being achieved elsewhere but:

a)   in a different way, or
b)   in another department, or
c)   by other members in your team or
d)   that in this fast-moving environment the result is simply no longer required. I once asked a manager why he completed, copied and distributed a report every week and he responded that he had been asked to do it several years before, so he still did it. No-one ever read the report.

Coming up with answers to the question "How can I reduce the time taken to zero?" will be quite difficult at first, but just as with the previous Steps, practice makes perfect. So let's start with a familiar large user of time from Step 1 - meetings. Companies and organisations have a large number of regular meetings - daily, weekly, monthly, yearly, but very rarely does anyone stop to consider if they are really necessary at all.

We've discussed ways of reducing the time taken on meetings, but why not try Step 3 thinking and eliminating some entirely?

Ask yourself the following questions about some of the meetings you arrange/attend:

– Is it really necessary for you to attend? Do you just sit there every week not saying a word because the discussion doesn't concern you?

– If you want to know what was discussed, can you just be asked to be added to the list of people receiving the minutes?

– For training purposes, is there an assistant in your department who would consider it a promotion to be asked to attend on your behalf?

– Could you ask to be called in when something is discussed that affects your department?

– This meeting has been going on for years on a weekly basis. What is it trying to achieve and is it succeeding? Is there another, more efficient way of achieving its objective? Could it be switched to fortnightly with no loss of effectiveness?

– Could two separate meetings be rolled in to one?

Now take a look at the last three meetings you arranged or attended and see if you can find a Step 3 solution and eliminate a meeting. As with Steps 1 and 2 it's perfectly OK not to find one, but by doing this exercise you will start training yourself to look for Step 3 eliminations.

Name of meeting	Possible Step 3 solution
Name of meeting	Possible Step 3 solution
Name of meeting	Possible Step 3 solution

You will encounter objections from many people because they like the safe and secure, we've-always-done-it-this-way approach. Don't ride roughshod, but start to influence your colleagues that they might consider another way. Don't jump in too quickly, prepare your arguments carefully and choose to speak to those who you think will be open to new ideas first.

Easier still - take a long hard look at your own meetings, and others may well see the benefits of your approach.

Now do the same for the last 3 emails you sent and the last 3 phone calls you made.

– Are you seeing the recipient soon (perhaps at a meeting that you couldn't eliminate) when the information could be imparted with no extra time taken?

– was it really necessary for the recipient to have the information you imparted? Is it useful to him/her; does the information ever get acted upon?

Email subject	Possible Step 3 solution
Email subject	Possible Step 3 solution
Email subject	Possible Step 3 solution

Telephone call subject	Possible Step 3 solution
Telephone call subject	Possible Step 3 solution
Telephone call subject	Possible Step 3 solution

Remember it is perfectly OK if you don't find a Step 3 solution in only three attempts. After some practice, if you could eliminate one in ten activities you would save yourself a considerable amount of time.

We now turn our attention to general tasks. Exactly the same applies to these; you should be looking for Step 3 solutions. By way of example, let's look again at that report that you need to compile every week (see Example 5). You've been compiling this report for years. We tried to find ways of completing the work more quickly. But using Step 3 thinking, try:

– Can I beg/cajole/bribe with lunch the computer department to produce the information in the form of a new print-out, thereby reducing your workload to a press of a button? The initial time spent by the computer department will be more than off-set by the continuing time savings every time you run the report - and anyway, it's one of the main functions of the computer department to produce effective reports.

– Is there an up and coming assistant who would relish the opportunity to complete the report for you? They would regard it as gaining more influence in the organi-sation, and would welcome the opportunity. The point is not to simply re-distribute all your work to other people, but to use it for training purposes.

– Can I combine this report with another one that is already being done e.g. combine a sales report with a margin report and make one sales and margin report? Much of the information will be duplicated, resulting in one of the reports disappearing completely.

– Should the report become a request-only report i.e. you will compile it whenever it is requested (which usually means more infrequently than at present)?

You will find it easier to establish Step 3 thinking in your own organisation (than in this example) because you know the people, the culture and dynamics. You'll know who needs information as opposed to who just wants it, but never uses it. The key thing is to simply pose the question. It's amazing how many tasks can be eliminated without - and this is key - harming the organisation. It is important that it is understood that Step 3 is not advocating the cutting of corners or the cessation of key tasks.

The opportunities for finding a Step 3 solution are fewer than with Steps 1 and 2, but each one has the potential to save a lot of time, especially if you eliminate a daily or weekly task. And as you get better at spotting Step 3 opportunities, so you will be moving much closer to your objective of getting on top of your work, and staying there.

We now have 3 of the Steps to consider simultaneously. Step 1 clearly only refers to three specific activities, phone calls, emails and meetings. If you have been following the examples and techniques you should be starting to use Step 1 easily and effectively. If not, forget about Steps 2 and 3 for the time being and concentrate on getting Step 1 working properly.

The relationship between Steps 2 and 3 is less clear cut. Which do you choose to tackle a task?

The answer lies in how far you have progressed through the Steps. If you are just starting out on step 3, you are probably best advised to apply Step 2 and have Step 3 in the back of your mind to see if anything occurs to you. If you've already been applying Step 3 for some time, then perhaps you could try applying Step 3 first, and if nothing comes quickly to mind then go for a Step 2 solution. If you are still unclear about your approach, re-read and review some of the examples in each step to get you back on track again, thinking in this new way.

The important thing is to have a framework and not to stick to a rigid formula. Sometimes a Step 2 solution will come quickly, sometimes a Step 3 solution will pop into your head immediately. Either way, the Step Method will be doing its job, saving you valuable minutes and hours.

Most people work for a lifetime and are never exposed to Step 3 thinking. You are now in a position to take advantage of its considerable strength and take a huge leap forward in the amount of work that you can get through in a day.

And don't forget to put that secret article on your desk to keep reminding yourself to think in this new way.

Helpful Pointers and other examples

There follows a series of examples showing different types and methods of eliminating tasks. Some will not be relevant to your particular field, but they all demonstrate the type of thinking that you will need to develop to get the maximum benefit from Step 3.

Example 10. Using technology to eliminate tasks

I came across a service business which became expert at Step 3 thinking. The business model meant that customers phoned a call centre to request the service, the call centre took a requested date and time for the independent service agent to call, and then phoned a service agent to confirm their availability and book the appointment. The call centre then called the customer back to tell them that the appointment was confirmed.

That's the way it worked when mobile phones were just becoming popular. The boss of the company had the vision to foresee that soon everyone would have a mobile phone and then applied Step 3 thinking to his business model. If all the service agents had mobile phones, then as the call centre inputted the customer details with the date and time for the appointment, the computer could automatically text the service agent with the name, address, date and time. The service agent just texted back with a "yes" or "no", completely eliminating the need for the call centre to call the service agent. Great Step 3 thinking.

Encouraged by this development he thought there must be a way to eliminate other tasks, and turned his attention to the call-back to the customer to confirm the appointment. If each customer who used the service had to have a mobile phone (which was already the case for the vast majority of his customers), then why not programme his computer to automatically re-route the yes or no text directly to the customer? When the text was being re-routed, the service agent's name and phone number could be added, thereby achieving his goal of completely eliminating the return call to the customer. Brilliant.

Now the only thing the call centre did was receive the customer phone call and enter the details on the central computer; he had eliminated a huge amount of work and cost. It would be great if he could eliminate this final task in the call centre but think and analyse as much as he did, he realised that it would be impossible to eliminate this task.

A while later, when the boss's phone was up for renewal he, along with the rest of the world upgraded to a smart-phone. Could this new technology provide a solution to his problem of tying to eliminate the need of using a call centre to take and input the service requests? Can you work out how he did it?

If everyone would eventually have a smart-phone, then everyone had access to the internet (as well as their home/work computers). If the request for the service could only be done via the internet, then it would already have been inputted. If he could then programme his computer to pick out the relevant parts of the inputted request, and convert it to a text message, it could be sent directly to a service agent. The rest of the process was already automated. Step 3 thinking had completely eliminated the need for his staff to be involved with the process of arranging service appointments. The business is now ten times the size it was, and the same call centre staff are still there, but they now spend their time helping to grow the business.

Example 11. Eliminating Deadlines

There are some tasks that you have that simply cannot be avoided. This example shows that you don't always have to tackle the problem head-on. Look to see if a similar situation exists in your company or organisation:

Filling out the monthly reporting is one of those jobs we all hate. It is very time specific and everything else stops for it. Of course you **always** get yours in on time, but how to do it without upsetting your peak efficiency?

When I worked for the American conglomerate Sara Lee, they had the most demanding schedule of reporting that I had come across. The worldwide figures had to be completed for publication one week (5 working days) after the month end. This meant that the European figures had to be consolidated 3 days after the end of the month, which meant that the UK's figures had to be sent no later than the end of day 2 after the end of the month. These figures included a complete P+L, balance sheet, cash flow and re-forecast for the remainder of the year.

You can imagine the strain this schedule put on the business. Nothing else was done by any department for two days and we worked late into the night to ensure the figures went in on time.

I had implemented Step 2 in order to create as much time as possible to complete the reporting but we were still under too much pressure to do what was required. Using Step 3 thinking, I couldn't eliminate the reporting or eliminate the deadline, but I could eliminate the starting date.

The next time we had a good month, we stopped all financial activity 3 days early. And then did the same every month. We still had the same number of working days in each month, they were just 3 days earlier than the calendar month (with the added benefit of 3 very useful extra days just before the year end, which was inflexible).

The effect was dramatic. Everyone had time to do the month end without disrupting their busy schedule and peak efficiency was maintained. The UK also got a reputation for always having the figures in on time and **never** having to be chased - unlike just about every other country.

Now look at your own circumstances. Are you being put under time pressure that is causing you problems? Could this type of Step 3 solution help? Make a note of any ideas that come to mind:

Type of time pressure	Possible Step 3 solution
Type of time pressure	Possible Step 3 solution
Type of time pressure	Possible Step 3 solution

If you can come up with just one idea here, you will be saving yourself and the organisation a lot of time and effort.

Example 12. Eliminating objections to buying in sales presentations

Again, another variant of elimination - this time one of the keys of successful selling - the elimination (rather than the usual handling) of objections in sales presentations. Even if you have no interest in sales, it's relevance is huge in all areas of business and organisations. It is likely that most of us will sooner or later have to sell something to colleagues or customers and it will probably be ideas or projects, rather than products. The same principles apply:

Every salesperson/sales manager has been there many times - you make your presentation, the buyer comes back with some objections, you handle them well but he has some more. The pros and cons go back and forth and the final result could go either way. Then finally he signs on the dotted line and you come out and punch the air. Now that, you say to yourself, is real selling at its best.

Not in my book.

The huge tussle described above should never have taken place. An onlooker to **your** sales presentation should go away thinking "that was easy, anyone could do that"

It needed Step 3 (eliminating tasks altogether) thinking. How could I stop the objections to buying flying across the table at me? The answer, and the secret of all sales presentations is knowledge - knowledge that is very easily but in fact rarely, obtained. To make a successful presentation, you must first:

– know your products inside out. Know everything they can do and everything they can't. Know what they're made of, how they were manufactured, why the packaging is the way that it is etc etc. If you don't already know this, take yourself off the road for a week, find a quiet office and learn it all parrot fashion. Then:

– know exactly the same information about your competitors' products.

– know every channel of distribution, and who sells which brands and which products

– know the retail price of all your products in every major customer, and the same for your competitors products.

Armed with this information in your head, put together your presentation, together with your suggested range of products and with some realistic pricing. As you go through your presentation with the buyer, there should be none of the objections that came up in my very first example. **You should have thought of every possible objection** before you started writing your presentation, and gently smoothed them away before they could be voiced by the buyer. The presentation becomes more of a conversation about the market, rather than a sales pitch. The key word is authority. You must speak and act with authority and the buyer will recognise it instantly. Every day buyers have sales people in their offices spouting off about their products, and who have no idea that the sales person's competitors have them cheaper, or better or more suited to his requirements. The buyer can't get rid of them quickly enough. When faced with someone who really knows what he is talking about..........he listens.

This is why I said that an onlooker would think that this selling game is dead easy. The buyer has no objections, he respects your knowledge and signs on the dotted line.

If you are customer facing, think about your own knowledge. If you really know your stuff, then you should be able to put together a range of products, at the right price and margin for your customers, and you will speak with authority.

If you do not need to sell products, but projects and ideas, can you speak with authority? Have you worked out all the objections that will come your way?

So whether it's products, projects or ideas where you need to try and eliminate objections, try completing the table for one such event that you have in your diary:

Event (products/project/ideas/other)	Objections to be eliminated

Without doubt you will now stand a better chance of getting the result that you need.

By now, the Step method will be saving you large amounts of time, and when you catch up with your workload, it's a liberating feeling.

What is just as important is that this will result in you "creating" more time. It's worth re-looking at what to do with this extra time as people react in different ways. Are we going to use this new time effectively? We also need to ask: "Is Parkinson's Law a reality and does it come in to play?"

Parkinson's Law states that work expands to fill the time available. Although it is presented in a humorous way, most of us will have experienced this effect to a greater or lesser degree. Many of us never look closely enough at the way we work to question whether Parkinson's Law is important or not. Well I can tell you that you don't have to spend time doing the analysis, there is no doubt about it, work **does** expand to fill the time available and most of us fit into the "greater" rather than the "lesser" category. Hopefully embarking on the Step method will have highlighted this point to you already, and we need to find a method of overcoming its effects.

As you should be operating Step 2 by now, then you will be looking for the fastest way of completing any given task. Parkinson's Law would therefore affect you only in one of two ways. Either

a)   as the outstanding tasks become fewer, you start to slow down, or

b) not knowing what to do with this new-found time, new tasks will appear to absorb it.

To ensure that you do not succumb to the affects of Parkinson's Law we must address each point:

a) As the outstanding tasks become fewer you start to slow down - The Step Method has an in-built antidote to this problem. Nothing new is required, just follow Step 2 diligently. Step 2 requires that you find the quickest way for **every** task. There is no link to the number of tasks outstanding. If you are on your very last task, step 2 requires you to find the quickest way to do it. This overcomes the problem. It's worthwhile noting, however, that what Parkinson is pointing out is part of human nature and Step 2 is making you overcome what would normally come naturally.

b) not knowing what to do with this new-found time, new tasks will appear to absorb it - here the Step method does not provide an automatic solution. As Parkinson's Law is pointing out human nature, then we need positive action to overcome it.

Choose from the following list, one or more suggestion(s) that fits your individual requirements:

1. Take 1 complete hour when you cannot be interrupted. Make a wish-list of things you would like to achieve (but have never had the time to even think about). You will find this much more difficult to do than you think. For most, if not all of our organisational life, we have done what is in front of us and have never been in a position to think of new ideas. Once you've

completed the list, re-write it, putting the items in order. Which order depends on your individual requirements, but one of the following could be a good starting point:

– by most profitable to the organisation
– by most important for your career development
– by most enjoyable
– by speed (ie the quickest first)

If this doesn't give you your final list, use it as a good starting point, and then mix and match the priorities and have (for example) a career development item at No1, then an enjoyable item at No2 and so on. Once you have your wish list in place, start at the top and use the Step method to ensure that you move through your list quickly and efficiently.

2. Utilise Steps 2, and 3 to pre-empt work that will be needed to be done in the future. You will find that the overall time taken to do a task will be reduced the earlier you start it. For example if you're planning a major meeting in 4 months time, and you would ordinarily start working on it 6 weeks beforehand, start the work now. Everyone will be available that far in advance, whereas if you send out invitations 6 weeks before, some will already be booked up, or you may even have to spend time re-scheduling. If you need information from other departments then the chances are that ordinarily you need to spend time chasing them to send it to you. If you've started 4 months before, then even if they are late returning the information, you will not need to spend time

chasing them (remember you're only looking to save a few minutes). Starting a task earlier will take away any time pressure that arises on many tasks, enabling you to work more efficiently and usually think more clearly. It's my experience that the earlier you start most tasks, the more efficient you will be completing it, thereby using your free time to create more free time.

3. Go home earlier than normal whenever possible. Take up that hobby you've always wanted to do and spend some time with your family.

Now choose 1, 2 or 3 and follow it.

Conclusion

At the beginning of Step 3, eliminating tasks altogether must have seemed fanciful, but by now you should have started doing it yourself and will be able to see the huge jump forward that will be possible when Step 3 becomes second nature.

Step 3 will give you fewer opportunities to save time, but on each occasion you eliminate a task, your saving will not be just a few minutes. Step 3 will give you substantial savings every time you can do it, and of course once the task has been eliminated you save every time you would have done it in the future.

These savings of time now need to be added to the savings from Step 1 and Step 2.

Cumulatively the effects are dramatic.

Remember:

At the beginning I stated that it is best to master the step you're on before moving on to the next one.

Ask yourself:

– Have I been able to eliminate many tasks?

– do I think of eliminating tasks every day?

– am I saving extra time (in addition to the time saved every day using steps 1 &2)?

If the answer to any of these questions is "no" then spend time concentrating on Step 3 before moving on to Step 4.

Training your department/division/company

Steps 1, 2 and 3 will have already changed your day from chasing your tail, to being able to be pro-active in deciding the course of your business, organisation or department. Remember that you're pretty good at getting things done quickly and efficiently now - but also remember that you've only been thinking like this for a relatively short period of time. You will find that you will get better and better at it, as you use the Step Method more.

If we are already doing all this, the next problem presents itself: can anything further be done to make an appreciable saving of valuable time?

Step 4 answers this question. Not only that, Step 4 has the potential of saving you more time than the first 3 steps added together.

It sounds incredible, but it's absolutely true.

You are just one person in your organisation. However efficient you become, it's unlikely that you will be able to seriously improve your organisation's efficiency and overall profit levels. But the Step method needs to do just that and Step 4 addresses this point.

Your professional achievements are not just the results **you** achieve, but more importantly the results of the people that work under you in your team. If they are not performing, then however good your own personal abilities, your results will never be anything but second-class. In many ways, it's our ability to manage people, getting the very best from them, that defines our success in business/professional life.

So if the Step method has transformed the way you work, creating time for you to be pro-active, why wouldn't it work for the people who report to you? Why wouldn't they get on top of their workload and start being pro-active? In fact can you imagine the effect on your depart-ment's results if everyone was on top of their work and coming up with new ways to improve the effectiveness of the department? Or just simply having more time to increase contacts with new customers (sales) or dream-ing up effective promotional campaigns (marketing) or coming up with reports that really help top management understand what is happening in their organisation (finance).

As you have now completed Steps 1, 2 and 3, Step 4 requires you to find a way to pass on the benefits of the Step method to members of your team. It is very important that you learn from your own experiences and pass on these benefits. In many ways, it is much easier to teach others than it is to teach yourself. This is because everyone learns the Step system at a different pace. Your pace was dictated by how quickly you decided to move through the book, irrespective of how you were grasping the fundamentals and how quickly you were mastering each Step. You are now in a position to dictate and control the exact speed that members of your team learn the Step Method. Expose them to Step 1 and monitor their progress. My experience is that they will want to get on to Step 2 before they have mastered Step 1, and if you also find this then simply don't reveal Step 2 until they are ready. Likewise with the subsequent Steps. This controlled method of learning and using the Step Method, coupled with passing on your own personal experiences, will mean that your team should be running effectively relatively quickly. Please remember though, that it's not a race. It's far more important to reach the end effectively, than to reach the end quickly but not be able to operate the Step Method efficiently and correctly. As you might expect by now, Step 4 is best explained by the use of examples.

If you do not have any people working under you in a team then take the opportunity to help your friends and colleagues. If they haven't read the book, then the chances are that their only exposure to the Step Method will be what you tell them, and Step 4 will certainly help them.

Implementing the Step Method in your Team

If you have a small number of people in your team - say eight people - you need to decide whether to introduce the Step Method to people individually or to the whole team together. I would recommend that you start with one person. Take them aside and explain that you intend training them to achieve more during the working day. Explain that you have tried the Method yourself and can guarantee that you will be able to save the person valuable minutes from day 1.

Explain to them Step 1. The exact way you do this will depend on the personality of the person you are talking to. One of the best ways is to buy them a copy of the book, but don't give it to them yet. Photocopy a few of the pages from Step 1 (especially the fill-in tables), and use these as visual aids to your explanation. They will need the book later to get full benefit from all the detail of the examples, but that can wait. You don't want them looking up and concentrating on Step 2 tomorrow !! Tell them about your own experiences and the things that worked particularly well for you. When you think they've got it, tell them to get started straight away with the exercises and then pitch straight in to the implementation (unless either you or they want to calculate the time saved by measuring current Step 1 activities)................and don't forget to explain about the secret object on the desk.

Best results have been achieved by the person being shown the Step Method not explaining what he/she is doing to colleagues, but by just getting on with it. Obviously if asked about it there is no point in denying they are implementing the Step Method, but there is no reason to advertise the subject. The trainee should just quietly get on and implement Step 1. The reason for this is that he/she doesn't want to waste all the time they've saved discussing it with colleagues - whose time will come later. Also someone may be upset that they were not chosen first and try to discredit your implementation.

You should monitor on a regular basis how the person is implementing Step 1. Remember that this is the first person you have trained in the Step Method and it's a learning curve for you too. When the first person is starting to get to grips with it, move on to the rest of the team either singly or in groups, using what you have learnt from training the first member of your team, and more importantly what you learned from your own implementation.

What about if you have more than one layer of management reporting to you - how should you implement the Step Method?

It would be very difficult indeed to introduce the Step Method to an entire medium or large size company in one go. I would recommend that you introduce it to one layer of management at a time, starting at or near the top of the organisation. Alternatively it could be introduced at a level where there is currently a lot of bottlenecks which are choking the company.

Whichever level you start with, the people involved need to start at the beginning of Step 1 and work their way through the steps, not attempting to train others until Step 3 has been completed.

Whoever starts the Step Method wants to progress as quickly as possible. Having seen the benefits of Step 1 everyone wants to know more. It is important to say again that everyone starting the Step Method must be proficient in one Step before moving on to the next Steps. Train individually or in small groups and don't make company announcements that some people will be introducing a new time management system - just get on and do it. Our first example gives an insight into some specific techniques used to overcome a whole department being behind in their work.

Example 13. Training a department in the Step method

I became the Director of an international marketing department that had 10 Marketing and Product Managers plus support staff, based in Paris. On speaking to everyone on joining, they all had the same complaint which could be summed up as "this is not a marketing department, there is no strategic planning, we all spend our time processing the paperwork to get a few new products launched each year for individual countries". This is a very common problem the world over and one that you should expect to experience whatever country you work in.

I explained to them that I could guarantee that the entire department would be on top of its workload and that as soon as that happened, we would go out for a departmental slap-up lunch, followed by a strategy meeting (the first for years).

I started with the three most senior people and they had little problem understanding and implementing Step 1. After allowing them time to become proficient, we moved on to Step 2. Explaining Step 2 in a classroom situation is easy enough (after all you've been through it yourself) but they were more sceptical over Step 2 than Step 1. If you meet this problem there are two options: either let them discover the effectiveness of Step 2 themselves, or give them plenty of actual examples relating to their own workloads. In this case, as we needed a swift outcome, I chose the latter. I sat alongside each one for a few hours watching how they worked. They were senior marketing and PR managers and were a bit unnerved at having their new boss watch them work. I stressed that I was not assessing what they did in any way, just how they did it. In addition, my promise of being able to get them developing marketing strategy, instead of pushing paper all day, meant they would be stupid not to give it a try. They each operated at different speeds and efficiency, but I gathered enough examples to prove to them individually that Step 2 was the way to get them back on top of their workload.

We then followed the standard Step Method, with me doing the training until the senior members of the team reached Step 4, when they took over. If there is any doubt in your mind that it works in English but not in other languages, then this example will change your mind. Even when I couldn't understand much of what was being said (my French was not good), I saw the results. Everything went according to plan - it's exactly the same in any language.

I'm sure you've guessed it by now - two months later we had that lunch and the first of many strategy meetings. This is a practical example of what can be achieved and will hopefully convince you that if it's been done before, then there's no reason why it shouldn't be done again - but this time by you.

When starting any member of the team on the Step method, you have one big advantage - the person learn-ing it will almost certainly gain substantial amounts of time from **day 1**. Demonstrating results so quickly and definitively will give your team the confidence to want to try the subsequent Steps.

As with all experience, having been through it, you'll be in a better position to train others. You'll remember that you went several days slipping back into your old way of working before you noticed that your colleague had borrowed your stapler (the secret object on your desk reminding you to follow the Steps). It's just this sort of experience that you can pass on to your team to enable them to go through the Steps more easily.

Your immediate goal is to get yourself up to date, and then your team. But what about bottlenecks in another part of the organisation? How many times have you been prevented from achieving your goals because someone in another department doesn't have the time to complete their part of the programme?(If it's anything like the companies I've worked in, both small and large, then often.)

Go and see the person who is holding everything up and discuss your project with them. During the course of the conversation you will easily be able to ascertain whether he or she really is overworked because anyone who feels that they have been given too much to do, is happy to tell the world. Whilst explaining the importance of your project and their part in the chain of people involved in it, drop in to the conversation the fact that you know exactly how they feel as you had been put in the same situation yourself. You should mention how the Step Method got you out of it, and pass on as little or as much information about it as the person wants.

You may be told to get lost and mind your own business, but that is not usually the reaction you will receive. People are generally interested to hear what you have to say and there is a good chance they'll give it a go. You'll also probably get the information you needed much more quickly than would have otherwise been the case.

Another breed of person altogether, however, is the professional "blocker". They seem to be around less and less these days, but nothing new gets passed them. The best advice I can give is do everything you can to avoid them. Try to avoid confronting them head-on. They've had years of experience of stopping change and they are hard to shift. If avoidance is not possible, get as much support from other members of the team before going on the offensive. Strength in numbers is your safest weapon.

Helpful Pointers and Other Examples

The following examples show the integration of the different steps with different management techniques. The first one is a combination of Steps 3 and 4:

Example 14. Solving Your Team's Problems

I once read a management book that had a chapter entitled "The most effective sentence in management efficiency". Eager to improve my abilities in this area I read on with anticipation. The chapter dealt in detail with the amount of time managers spend sorting out problems generated by their teams. It is very time consuming having people constantly putting their heads round the door and asking for advice. Of course this a major part of a manager's job, and care must be taken not to give the impression that you don't want to be disturbed - but if the number of occasions can be reduced, then a lot of valuable time will be saved.

The magic sentence the book said you should say when this happens is: "What do **you** think is the best solution?"

This made perfect sense to me, encouraging people to think through problems and in many cases come to a sensible conclusion with minimal input from you.

Margaret Thatcher changed my thinking completely. She had a Business Secretary, Lord Young, and when describing his abilities said "He brings me solutions, not problems".

Brilliant - instead of asking your team how to deal with a problem, encourage them to come to you with their problem, but always accompany it with their best guess solution. The more they do it, the better they become at problem solving resulting in them needing to consult you on fewer occasions. It therefore follows that you will be spending less and less time on this part of your job.

Step 3 and Step 4 thinking at its finest.

But what if you are not a manager and you don't experience this problem? This example is still very relevant to you, and is a marvellous pointer as to how you could change the way you approach problems and save time. Why not become a "Lord Young" yourself and get a reputation for always bringing solutions, not problems, to your boss? This is still classic Step 3 thinking (but this time it's eliminating your boss's problems, not yours). The more you do it, the better you will become at solving problems and you will save time by not having to interrupt your boss so often.

This can even be taken a stage further. Why not combine both ideas? Many people are in a chain of command, with some people reporting to them and they themselves are part of a team reporting to their boss. If you are in this position, why not combine the two aspects above and encourage your team to bring solutions, not problems and in addition you do the same with your boss? A perfect scenario, where everyone wins.

The next example will show how to save a considerable amount of time using a combination of Steps 2, 3 and 4, and it uses the Steps to challenge conventional wisdom.

Example 15. How to Delegate

There is a well known management philosophy called "Delegation and Follow- up". I was taught this as a management trainee in my very first job.

It says that as a manager, you need to delegate to your team all the necessary jobs to achieve your and their objectives. It also assumes that the person who is supposed to do the delegated task may not complete it, or may not do it in the correct way. Therefore the manager should check that the task has been completed correctly (the follow-up), thereby ensuring the smooth operation of the department.

All very sensible, and this technique has been used for decades by managers to ensure that everything under their responsibility is completed satisfactorily.

I too operated this system for many years, and became a successful manager using it. And then I started Step 2 thinking (finding the quickest way). I asked myself: "why am I spending so much time ensuring that my team complete all their tasks?" My first answer was "because that's the way I was taught, and the way everyone else does it".

Step 3 thinking (eliminating tasks altogether) sent me in a different direction. I came to the conclusion that this activity **could** be eliminated without any adverse affect to the team's performance. Simply speak to each member of your team, either individually or as a team, and explain that they are all responsible people and that if you ask them to complete a task, you will no longer check that it has been completed....you will assume it has been completed and will leave it at that. Explain that if the task has **not** been completed (for whatever reason, valid or not) they should simply let you know that it wasn't completed and give you the time when it will be completed.

The effect is staggering. Firstly you save a huge amount of time by not having to constantly check that tasks have been completed. Secondly none of your team will want to admit to you that they were unable to complete a task on time, so will shift heaven and earth to ensure it **is** completed on time. The department's efficiency will improve and everything gets done on time. And don't forget that you have tasked your team with Step 2 thinking so that they find the quickest way **without sacrificing quality.** They will understand that the job you have given them to do must be completed in the expected time-frame, to the expected quality standard. It is not acceptable to be on time but below standard.

You will have to make an example of anyone who does not complete a task on time and does not tell you. Everyone will become aware of this and make sure that it doesn't happen to them.

Result: more things get done on time and you have much more time for the things that really matter. It's a very effective management tool.

When training, don't forget that your team were not made in your image. They will have different personalities and specialities and you must recognise this and adjust your training accordingly. I learned this when I first became a sales manager. "Just teach the team how to do it the (successful) way I do it" I thought. I then recruited a young guy who turned out to be the best salesman I have ever met.

He tried selling the way I taught him (my way) and he failed miserably. When he did it his way, he was extremely successful. It turned out that I sold on reasoned argument and technique, and he sold on his personality and charm. He couldn't sell the way I did it and I couldn't sell the way he did it - though we were both very successful. Bear this in mind while completing any training - not just the Step Method.

Conclusion

If you are a manager then you will be responsible for the ongoing development of the people that report to you. Your team's result will definitely start to improve as each member becomes more efficient (how could they not?).

So you can see that if your whole department is now applying the Step Method, the effects will be dramatic and you can now see why I made the statement that Step 4 can be more beneficial than the previous steps put together.

But take it a stage further.

Do the people who report to you have people reporting to them? If so, when you are satisfied that they have got the hang of it, why wouldn't they train the people who report to them in the benefits of the Step Method?

Can you imagine the results, if you are a divisional manager, and your whole division is working like this? Or if you are a Managing Director, that the whole company is working like this?

THE 4 STEPS

Step 1 - Saving time communicating
Step 2 - Finding the quickest way, without sacrificing quality
Step 3 - Eliminating tasks altogether
Step 4 - Training your dept./division/company

We conclude by reviewing some important points and giving some extra background information.

You have now completed reading about the 4 Steps and you have been introduced to a time management system that guarantees to save you time, starting on day 1. Keep using the Step Method and the results become cumulative.

The Step Method will always gain you extra time, but in order to maximize the time gained, do not go through the Steps too quickly. Take your time. It's not a race and you will gain maximum benefit by mastering one Step before taking on a new one. The reasons for not moving on too quickly have nothing to do with your management abilities but everything to do with focus. If you attempt to implement all four stages simultaneously, you will probably fail to achieve any significant result. It is simply impossible to think in so many directions at once.

So to avoid grinding to a halt, train yourself as you will have to train your team, one Step at a time. And anyway, as with every aspect of management, if you are going to train your team, you need to be an expert yourself, so take time to master each Step before moving on. It's key to the success of the Step Method.

We turn now to the question of relevancy - "This all sounds very good but it doesn't really apply to me or the organisation where I work." My answer is that I have **never** come across a business or organisation where the Step Method would not be beneficial.

Don't fall into the trap of thinking that the Step Method only works for managerial positions. Manual jobs lend themselves wonderfully to Step Method thinking and you should be eagerly seeking out ways of saving time. Don't spend valuable time trying to work out whether The Step Method is going to work for you or your team - just get started implementing the Steps in turn and the benefits will come. And don't think to yourself that the Step Method would work for only a part of your duties and not the rest. It is relevant to **every** part of your job.

Step method thinking also works on production lines - where the efficiency gains can be measured accurately (the system of calculation is complex and not relevant here).

The point is that major efficiency gains can be made by following the Step Method in most, if not all, manual processes and jobs. The main focus is on Step 2 (finding the quickest way without sacrificing quality) and Step 3 (eliminating tasks completely). The chances are that it's been some time since someone looked at the processes with new eyes, specifically looking for efficiency improvements. And the chances are that the person who last took a look at it was not as proficient as you. Remember, if you are already using Step 3 (eliminating tasks completely) then you have spent weeks or months finding quicker ways of doing things. You probably will be more proficient than the last guy who looked at it, and will in all probability save your organisation a considerable amount of money.

I would go so far as to suggest that if you were to use the Step Method in any given job - let's say filling shelves or working the tills in a supermarket - by the end of the week, you would be offering new ideas to management of ways to improve the efficiency and quality of the service. These are bold words, but I have seen it done so many times I don't doubt that they are true.

This next example shows how the Step Method is very relevant, even when it is not expected to be so:

Example 16. The Step method relates to any job

I gave a working draft of this book to a pharmacist friend of mine - a bright guy with his own business - who was struggling to find the time to get all his work done. He was having to work later and later in the evenings and he felt he was having to run faster just to stay where he was.

After reading this working draft, his summary was that the Step Method would be very beneficial to anyone who worked in an office, and that there were some good ideas to help him, but the Step Method is not so relevant to someone who is dealing with customers in a shop all day long, and dispensing prescriptions. Being customer facing, and the fact that processing scripts was so mechanical, there was little room for improvement.

As we were talking, he was sorting out some papers for submission to the government.

He explained this was a good example - he had to speak to his customers, fill in the forms and submit the information by computer to the relevant government department. There was no getting away from it, his business would suffer considerably if the forms were not returned correctly, and on time. He had 1,500 forms to complete - each taking about 3 minutes - a total of 75 hours work, spread over the coming weeks. I explained that the Step system was in fact very relevant to a great deal of what he did every day, and that we should apply it to this 75 hr job.

Step 1 (saving time on phone calls and emails) was irrelevant as there was no phoning or emailing involved. So we turned our attention to Step 2 (finding the quickest way without sacrificing quality). As things stood, a member of staff had to describe the details of a new NHS system for the dispensing of prescriptions and try to get the patient to agree that it could be used on all their future prescriptions. Getting the patients agreement was proving to be more difficult than expected and very time consuming. If the patient agreed, and eventually most did, the staff member would go through the questionnaire with the patient, simultaneously filling out the form. The forms were then given to someone else who put the information on to the computer when time became available - usually after the shop had closed because everyone was too busy during the day. It was a simple enough process, he explained, but very time consuming and not much opportunity to use the Step Method to reduce the time taken.

After giving it some thought, I asked him "You have many members of staff, which one has the highest proportion of "Yes's" and what does she say to the patient" His answer was that he had one staff member whose conversion rate was excellent but it was impossible for her to talk to everyone - there were just too many patients. I explained that I bet she had a specific sentence or two that did the trick every time. He should find out what she said and instruct all the staff to use the same wording.

When he did this the following day the conversion rate increased and the time taken to convince the patient was dramatically cut. That member of staff had already "found the quickest way" for him.

I then turned my attention to Step 3 thinking and said to him "why not invest in some clip boards and while you are making up the prescription, give the form to the patient and they can fill it out themselves - it's a very straight forward form and in any event it will only take a few seconds for a staff member to check everything is correct.

This eliminated completely his staff's need to spend time filling out the forms. There was just the 30 seconds or so checking the form.

Turning my attention to the inputting of the information on to the computer, he stopped me and said that he got the picture and would work it out for himself at the shop the following day.

The combination of both measures resulted in a saving of at least half of the time required to complete the task - that's 37 hours - almost a complete week, stretched over the coming couple of months. As is demonstrated here, the Step Method is not a complicated management system. It was simply the fact that my pharmacist friend was not in the habit of "finding the quickest way without sacrificing quality" that prevented him from saving this time. This is why the Step Method is so useful - it's not revolutionary, you just have to train yourself to think in a slightly different way. I suggested to him that the extra time he had created for his staff should also give him some extra time as he could pass over some of his customer contact to his staff. He should use this extra time to do some more Step 2 thinking (finding the quickest way) and that he should take a least a couple of hours to take a step back and look at the strategic direction of his business - something he had not done for a long time.

I have given this example in detail to help convince you that you should not think that the Step Method is not so relevant to your situation.

It is.

Using the Step Method over time will surely make you more efficient, but how can you be absolutely certain?

There's one sure fire way of getting your answer to this question. Every once in a while, do you ask yourself "how come a couple of years ago, I seemed so busy but achieved so little?" Increasing your productivity is an on-going, life- long pursuit, one in which it is impossible to say that you have reached perfection. But you will, nevertheless, be able to see your improvements by looking back over your career. When doing this, always remember that you have not and must not sacrifice quality in your pursuit of efficiency.

You will indeed wonder why it was that, when you felt you were a hot-shot manager/employee a few years ago, looking from where you are now, you can see that you had plenty of improvements to make and you were in fact a bit slow. You will be able to see the difference in your management efficiency between then and now, and be able to see how far you have come.

Now a final **really** interesting bit..............

Look forwards, rather than backwards. You know how well you're doing now - how much work you can get through to the amazement of your colleagues? Well if you continue to work on your skills with the 4 Steps, in a couple of years time, you will look back at your working life today and wonder why it was that you were so slow at doing everything. You will have become much more efficient than you are today.

It's hard to imagine but is absolutely true.

Summary of Examples

About the Author

Peter Keen started his career in sales, and moved via marketing into General Management. He has worked for small UK companies, large multi-national companies, and small UK divisions of large multi-nationals, giving him a large breadth of experience. The companies have included General Foods (now Kraft), Revlon, Sara Lee Corporation and Alcatel.

His last corporate position was being involved in a management buyout of a loss-making division of the telecommunications giant Alcatel. This company was subsequently returned to robust health and floated on the French stock exchange. He later sold his complete shareholding and retired at 53 years of age.

After a 2 year break, Peter, together with an ex-colleague, launched a electronics accessories brand in the UK. This new company has been structured and is run completely on the Step Method, making it one of the most, if not the most, efficient company in its marketplace.

Peter lives in the UK and is married with 5 children.

Lightning Source UK Ltd.
Milton Keynes UK
UKOW04f0330101213

222675UK00001B/9/P